Bedford
Commercials
Of
The 1930s

Robert W. Berry

Nostalgia Road Publications

The Nostalgia Road Series™

is produced under licence by

Nostalgia Road Publications Ltd.

Units 5-8, Chancel Place, Shap Road Industrial Estate,
Kendal, Cumbria, LA9 6NZ
Tel.+44(0)1539 738832 - Fax: +44(0)1539 730075

designed and published by

Trans-Pennine Publishing Ltd.

PO Box 10, Appleby-in-Westmorland, Cumbria, CA16 6FA
Tel.+44(0)17683 51053 Fax.+44(0)017683 53558
e-mail:admin@transpenninepublishing.co.uk

and printed by

Kent Valley Colour Printers Ltd.

Kendal, Cumbria +44(0)1539 741344

© Trans-Pennine Publishing Ltd. 2004

Front Cover: *Part of the Vauxhall Heritage collection this 1931 2-ton WH model (which was registered in Bradford) has been used many times in Vauxhall/Bedford publicity material, nevertheless it makes an admirable illustration for the front cover of this book.* Vauxhall Motors

Rear Cover Top: *The Bedford Gathering 2002 played host to this WTL drop-side lorry, from the second generation of Bedford commercial vehicles. This up-rated the capacity to this much-needed 3-tons.* Matthew Richardson

Rear Cover Bottom: *Seen at the 2001 Goodwood Heritage Revival this 2-ton WH mobile fish and chip shop. This preserved example shows a popular use for Bedford chassis in the 1930s, and period illustrations can be found on pages 32 and 33.* Alan Earnshaw

Title Page: *An unusual method of delivering trucks, this image was to have been used on the cover of the proposed 1939 Bedford brochure. It was a true representation of how 'native' buses were supplied to Saudi Arabia, but as no Bedford cameraman was ever sent to this exotic location, the picture was 'comprised' from a variety of images in the design studio at Luton.*

INTRODUCTION

"History is Bunk!" or so said Henry Ford, but I disagree, with his sentiments, as his venerable Model T is without doubt not only part of history, but also the foundation of the worldwide Ford Motor Company empire today. In parallel, the British commercial vehicle manufacturer, Bedford, was throughout its long and historic life, a veritable cornerstone of the enormous General Motors Empire.

In the terms of the motor industry, history is very important and although much of it is recorded, occasionally little gems surface from time to time. Indeed, hidden in a cupboard in Dunstable for many years is one such example, namely the proof pages for the Bedford catalogue that was to be distributed at the various motor shows that were planned for the latter part of 1939 and early 1940.

Above: *From the beginning, Bedford endeavoured to build practical vehicles to cater for every demand of industry! Not only did you 'see them everywhere', but you also saw them in the most unlikely places as well. Above and left, a 1932 WHG model delivers sewer pipes on the rocky bed of the River Taff,*

This book has therefore been dedicated to this document, and it now appears (after a brief introduction), some 65 years after its publication was delayed by the outbreak of World War II in 1939.

The history of Bedford Goes back to 1931, but to unearth the foundations of the company you would need to go back to 1857. In this year, a Scottish engineer by the name of Alexander Wilson established an iron works in Wandsworth Road in the London suburb of Vauxhall, on the south bank of the River Thames.

Announcing
the

BEDFORD

2-TON TRUCK
LONG & SHORT WHEELBASE

(Full particulars on following pages)

Made *by* Vauxhall Motors Ltd.

The Bedford 2-Ton Truck

The long wheelbase Bedford fitted with cab and dropside body. Note the imposing appearance.

The photographs on either side show two views of the back axle, and give some idea of the extremely sturdy construction.

The short wheel-base chassis.

The business was involved in the production of engines and pumps for the growing maritime industry, but before long internal combustion engines supplanted the steam engines. Then, during 1903, the first Vauxhall motor cars were built alongside the company's other products. Car production proved so successful that a move to Luton in Bedfordshire took place in 1905.

Meanwhile, in America, William Crapo Durant, born in 1860 in Boston Massachusetts, was rapidly gaining a reputation as an entrepreneur. He owned the Durant – Dort Company, one of the largest manufacturers of horse-drawn vehicles in the world.

During 1904, 43-year-old Durant bought the Buick Automobile Company after an appeal by the Buick Directors, for although David Dunbar Buick, along with his engineer Walther Marr had designed and built the prototype Buick in 1903, it was not until August 1904 that the first production car was ready and sold.

Durant took over financial control of Buick in November 1904 and by 1908 he had completely turned Buick's fortunes around, so much so that by the end of the year Buick was among America's top four automobile manufacturers. Building on his success, Durant had looked around for other possible acquisitions during this time and had subsequently purchased Cadillac, Olds and Oakland, a company that was to be renamed Pontiac in 1926.

Henry Ford had also considered selling his company to Durant before development had started on the Model T, but Durant had been unable to raise the $8,000,000 asking price. Durant was satisfied, even without Ford as he now had the largest automobile manufacturing company; in 1909 it became collectively known as General Motors. At the time that Durant was starting to build his empire a man called Louis Chevrolet, one of seven children of a Swiss watchmaker, had come to America to make his fortune.

Left: *Illustrating part of a feature for the New Bedford 2-Ton trucks, was this view that appeared in the 'in-house 'General Motors News. It brings to potential customers attention, the imposing appearance and sturdy construction of the new truck.*

Top Right: *Austere bus bodywork crudely lengthened to fit the long wheelbase Bedford Chassis, these two vehicles were owned by Mr H.C. Simmons of Dover, and used to convey men to Betteshanger, Snowdon and Tilmanstone Collieries.*

Middle Right: *Although in their early days Bedford did not build large capacity commercial vehicles, their reputation for reliability and economy was such that large and small municipal authorities alike turned to Bedford for support vehicles, as this 1932 WHG tipper of Glasgow Corporation Transport shows.*

Bottom Right *Announced in 1932 the Bedford VYC Light 12-cwt van chassis was a replacement for the Chevrolet AC van. This model is clearly identified by the six small diameter wheel-studs, the heavier models having eight. Note too the small projecting hubs used on the first year's production vehicles.*

Chevrolet had arrived in the new world with two of his younger brothers and he was soon to make his mark in the motoring industry. He joined the Fiat agents Holland Tangeman in New York and during 1905 won his first motor race driving a Fiat. He then went on to become a very successful racing car driver and this brought him to the attention of William Durant, who offered him a position in the Buick racing team. Chevrolet was not only a successful racing car driver, but was also a very competent designer and engineer.

In fact he had successfully modified Buick-based racing cars before joining Buick. During the spring of 1911, Durant bought a garage and promised Louis Chevrolet sufficient financial backing to enable him to build cars. This was to bring about the establishment of the Chevrolet Motor Company which was incorporated in Detroit on 3rd November 1911. Sadly, because of the uneasy relationship between Durant and himself, Chevrolet left the company in 1913.

The company that took Chevrolet's name became part of Durant's General Motors empire in 1918 and although the company were producing commercial vehicles under the GMC label, Chevrolet became a very important artery in both car and truck production. As an aside, we might mention that the GMC organisation came about as the result of the consolidation of the 'Rapid Motor Vehicle Company', founded in Detroit in 1904 and the 'Reliance Motor Company' of Owosso, Michigan, founded in 1902. Of course, the North American market was the company's primary goal, but they had recognised that light commercial vehicles would have a potential overseas market, and Britain of course was an early target for export.

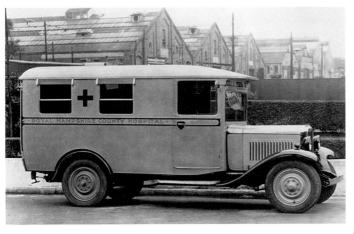

Top Left: *The direct replacement for the Chevrolet truck models was the Bedford WS model 30-cwt chassis, which was announced in April 1932. (Little Lizzie) here with her ornate rave boards and neat coach-lining would (unlike a lot of other Bedford's) have had a rather easy life transporting glass and china. Operating from Staffordshire, this little truck proved a reliable alternative to the more traditional mode of transport employed by local firms, namely canal barge or railway truck. Indeed, it was not just small pottery firms that used Bedford trucks for this work, as some of the larger, more illustrious companies, like Josiah Wedgwood were loyal customers for many years*

Middle Left: *Registered in Plymouth in 1932, this Bedford VYC 'rural school bus' owned by Messrs. R. Finch & Son of Princetown stands among the innocence of youth beneath brooding school walls. The scene is softened somewhat by a juvenile romantic! Many of the children pictured here were the sons or daughters of the warders at the nearby Dartmoor Prison.*

Bottom Left: *Admirably suited to the role of an ambulance with its very quiet six-cylinder engine, this 1932 Bedford WS model with its typical high waisted body of the period was one of many examples sold for such municipal duties as this.*

American-built 10-cwt commercial vehicles found a ready market in Britain during the 1920s but, as Chevrolet were quick to recognise, the 1-ton market was completely dominated by Ford. Ford had, after all, an established factory at Trafford Park in Manchester and a very sound product in the 1-ton Ford Model TT that had been introduced in 1917. Being designed as a commercial vehicle it was not subject to the horse-power tax, which rated the 2.9-litre engine of the conventional Ford Model T car at 23hp rating by the RAC. This was a system that favoured the use of smaller engine cars, and disadvantaged many of the manufacturers of that day. However, commercial vehicle taxation was related to the vehicle's weight (or in the case of public service vehicles, their seating capacity), so this market place was completely different to the car market and this allowed American companies a potentially good level of export opportunities.

General Motors took the courageous step to compete with Ford on their own ground by introducing a 1-ton Chevrolet for British users. Coincidentally, by doing this they they also avoid heavy import duties by building them in Britain using components brought into the country from General Motors' Canadian factory.

For this purpose a site was chosen and a new factory built at The Hyde, Hendon in North London and the assembly of British-built Chevrolet commercial vehicles began there in 1923. Two models were built, the car-based AB and the LQ models, which were of various vans and lorries up to a 25-cwt carrying capacity. These vehicles were powered by a four-cylinder overhead valve engine of 2,802 cubic capacities.

There was also a small number of buses built on the LQ chassis and other models that were in production from 1923 until the end of December 1928. December 1928 saw a revision of the range by the introduction of a more powerful six-cylinder power plant. The AB was replaced by the AC model of a 10-cwt capacity, while LQ models were able to take a 30-cwt payload. This new engine nicknamed the 'Stove Bolt 6' with its $3^5/16$ inch bores and 3 inch stroke provided a capacity of 3,180cc.

General Motors had already acquired Vauxhall by this time so the decision was made to move production to Luton and design and build from the outset commercial vehicles with the British Market in mind. New premises were built within the factory site at Luton; this work starting in 1929, in preparation for this, the 1930 edition of the instruction book refers to these models as being Luton-built.

The first Bedford models were shown in April 1931 and obviously had a lot in common with the successful Chevrolet. Two models were initially built, these being the WHG, which had the same wheelbase as the LQ 131 inches (10' 11"), and the longer WLG on a 157 inch (13' 1") wheelbase.

A degree of redesign had been incorporated to increase the capacity to 2-tons, but the visually obvious changes were the use of perforated disc wheels to aid brake cooling, and twin wheels on the rear axle. The new Bedford models had vertical bonnet louvres, extended to the full length of the bonnet side panels, whilst the radiator grill was redesigned and incorporated Vauxhall's Griffin emblem with the Bedford name.

When the commercial vehicles had become established, the company turned its attention to the public service vehicles market later that year. Before long two 'new' bus models appeared in the range, although these were very closely related to the commercial vehicle chassis. These were designated WHB, intended to carry 14-seat bus bodywork and the WLB, primarily designed as a 20-seat bus or coach.

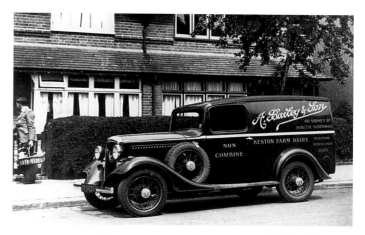

Top Right: *Introduced in 1933 was a new Bedford 8-cwt van, two types being available. The ASY with a 12hp engine of 1503cc, or the ASX with its 14hp 1,781cc six-cylinder engine. This is a 1933 Croydon-registered example of A. Bailey & Sons and used for door-to-door milk deliveries.*

Middle Right: *The advertising sentiment could very easily be coined (Ah Bedford or, Ah Beautiful), on this rear three-quarter view of the Bedford ASY/ASX 8-cwt van. Clearly this shows a very practical vehicle with tremendous advertising potential.*

Bottom Right: *Offering value for money at £155, the 8-cwt ASY model Bedford van was the cheapest six-cylinder goods vehicle on the market when purchased by the St. Albans Co-operative Society. The low purchase price and mechanical design being common to the car and van enabled this model to remain in production until 1939, five years longer than its car equivalent.*

Top Left: *A great many early bus companies started business with a vehicle that could be converted from fare carrying passengers to goods and back again. By 1930 this idea of a dual-use vehicle had all but died out, but here we have a Bedford WLB bus of W.V. Roberts of Petworth, Sussex, that continued this idea by means of some novel features.*

Middle Left: *The Bedford WLB featured above had a removable panel, incorporating the emergency exit at the back of his bus. Once this was lifted out and the seats removed, a tail-board could be put in place, and the boards fitted to the side windows. This allowed Mr. Roberts to operate what was effectively a large capacity goods vehicle for no extra outlay.*

Bottom Left: *After a passenger adaption of the WTL chassis was shown at the Scottish Motor Show in 1934, Bedford made a passenger vehicle designed around this the WTB. Illustrated here is a 1935 Bedford WTB with bodywork by Duple. The vehicle, registered with the West Riding of Yorkshire County Council plate AWR 97, is in the dark green and cream livery of Ezra Laycock of Barnoldswick, one of the County's oldest bus proprietors. Note the fact that the bus, on a Skipton - Colne service, is picking up lady passengers from outside a public hall that is staging All-In Wrestling!*

The very first Bedford bus completed in August 1931, with chassis number 100001, was a WHB model and carried 14-seat bus bodywork by the coachbuilder 'Waveney' of Oulton Broad, Lowestoft. Registered TM 9347 it was sold to John E. Woodham of Melchbourne, and was not withdrawn from active daily service until 1956. The WHB was powered by a six-cylinder petrol engine of 3.18 litres, transmission being through a single-plate clutch and a four-speed gearbox. Only 102 WHB models were ever constructed and of these, all but eight were delivered to the home market, whereas the WLB models reached 1,895 models built. Of these 1,431 were sold for use in Britain, the last one appearing in September 1935.

First appearing in 1934, the WTH and the longer wheelbase WTL models were of a semi-forward control desin and built to accomodate up to a three-ton payload. They were powered by the Bedford six-cylinder, 26.3hp petrol engine with a bore and stroke of 84.14mm x 95.25mm. Transmission was through a four-speed gearbox, single plate clutch and spiral beval rear axle.

January 1935 saw the appearance of a new bus chassis this was the WTB, which was basically the 27hp WLB model but with an extended chassis and wheelbase of 13' 11", which enabled a 26-seat body to be fitted, prior to this the WTL lorry chassis had been modified for this purpose. During 1936 the WT models were fitted with an all-metal cab and re-designed front wings and radiator shell. Then, in 1937, the original engine was replaced by a new six-cylinder, 27.34hp petrol engine.

This covered the first decade of Bedford's production, and whilst the WH and WL models were an undoubted step forward, they were still little more than basic updates of the Chevrolet models of the 1920s. Therefore, for the 1940s, a new range was required to meet the challenges, so Bedford devised a new series of commercials.

This new range had models within itself capable of different capacities, the K-Types were capable of 1-ton to 2-ton, the M-Types were suited for work in the two- to three-ton range, and the O-Types were designed with six three-to four-ton chassis, six five-ton chassis and a six- to eight-ton tractor and cab chassis.

To effectively promote its new range of truck and bus chassis, Bedford therefore looked at its previous success stories to produce a brochure entiled *You See Them Everywhere*. This booklet would have gone into print in October 1939 for full circulation in the period December 1939 to April 1940. However, at the time of its planning, the eventuality of war with Germany was far from being a certainty, even though the Luton works were being prepared for that eventuality.

The brochure that follows has been re-created faithfully from the original artwork, loaned by a donor who has asked to remain anonymous, but who had been part of the advertising team at Vauxhall in the period concerned. We have added nothing to the original captions, nor taken anything away, but we trust that this does not mean that readers will have problems in identifying the specific vehicles in the 1930s range.

It will be noted that Bedford's role as both a supplier of both export and municipal models is widely emphasised, as this showed the level of 'respectability' the company felt it had reached in under ten years effort!

Top Right: *Soon after the WTL and short wheel base WTH had gone into production in 1934 Bedford began to used the slogan 'You see them everywhere', and indeed you did, for the WT models added to the success and the WTH proved to be a market leader. With its stubby frame it proved to be ideal as a tipper and many civil engineering companies built up large fleets of them.*

Middle Right: *One of the very popular Bedford 2-ton WHG vans, this 1935 example registered in Darlington belonged to a gas company, and was probably one of the last of this type. Note will be made of the very familiar names in and around the grocer's window; OXO cubes, Brooke Bond Tea, and Black Cat Cigarettes.*

Bottom Right: *Now a look at the competition. This Hull based electricity company is also using a Bedford WHG, the short wheel base 2-ton truck of 1936 shows just how much the 2-ton and 30-cwt range was altered in the latter part of 1935, new cab, radiator, whilst the bonnet gained horizontal louvres, however the main mechanical units remained little changed.*

The book is therefore left as a tribute to the stage of development that the company had reached at the end of the 1930s, and shows how it had 'set out its stall' for the 1940s ahead. The fact this was never printed as intended at the time meant that a little piece of history was in danger of slipping quietly into oblivion. When the booklet was shown to me, I thought it was something that could be rectified, and I hope you agree with me.

It is quite impossible to try and guess where the company might have developed had not the war intervened. Yet it is staggering to think of just how much the company were involved with war production at Luton, and the 'shadow factory' that was later built at Dunstable. During the period 1939-1945, the huge Vauxhall car plant at Luton, Bedfordshire was turned over almost exclusively to military production. Not only did the company continue its range of Bedford commercials and PSVs, but it also extended to the manufacture of tanks, aircraft components and a miscellany of other war-related products. We have already covered post-war development in our book *Bedford Light Commercials of the 1950s & '60s*, and we hope to look at the war years in a later volume, but for now, we hope you enjoy this unique look at 1939.

Right: *A new engine and radiator grill were introduced in July 1938 to the larger models in the Bedford commercial vehicle range. The engine's volume went up to 3,519cc and the new radiator grill was of a bowed design, incorporating thin horizontal bars. Allied Dairies show here two of their new WS type 30-cwt vans, ARJ 822, and ARJ 823, while ARJ 818, a BYC 12-cwt model shows this type continued unchanged for a few months. The other Bedford BYC model seen in this picture, RJ 5605, dates from 1936.*

Below: *Bedford continued with their WTB bus chassis and this 13'11" wheelbase model that had been introduced in November 1935 proved very popular. The advent of the new coach touring market that rapidly blossomed during the mid-1930s was to create an insatiable demand for day outings' that even World War II found it hard to diminish. This illustration shows an example bodied by Willowbrook of Loughborough who was another company that enjoyed a lot of success in their own right. They supplied this luxury coach for W. Parsons of Stanton-Under-Bardon in Leicestershire. Note the sun-visor over the driver's window and the sliding sun roof above the passenger cabin - just right for a 'chara' trip in the 'season'.*

YOU SEE THEM EVERYWHERE!

The first Bedford was produced in 1931. Many of the vehicles sold in that year are still on the road. Yet, in the short time that has elapsed since they were built, the name and the trucks that bear it have penetrated into every trade and almost every corner of the world. In the United Kingdom today, approximately 40 per cent of the total number of vehicles sold in the carrying capacity classes in which Bedfords compete are Bedfords.

In the export market, Bedfords have accounted for nearly one half of all British-made trucks shipped to overseas countries for the last seven years. It has taken less than a decade to establish Bedford's reputation for reliability, economy and long life wherever transport is used. And the slogan 'You see them Everywhere' is known and accepted the world over, not as a copywriter's catch phrase but as a simple statement of fact.

In compiling this album, the chief object has been to illustrate the 'ubiquity' of the Bedford; to indicate the extraordinary wide range of uses to which it has been and can be put at home and abroad. The vehicles illustrated are not all up-to-date. They are selected, not to show the latest features of engine and chassis design, but to demonstrate the part that Bedford can play in every phase of industrial and social life. Whatever the job, in other words, there is a Bedford to do it. With this thought in the minds of all who represent Bedford, whether in the domestic or export market, the future should hold even greater successes than the past. We have proved that the Bedford can 'take it'. We have proved that it is dependable, economical to run and efficient over long periods of consistent hard work. And these photographs will help to prove that it is just as adaptable as it is dependable.

"In Times of War & Peace"

The three fighting services of Great Britain are all Bedford users.
This 15-cwt. Infantry Wagon is one of a large fleet specially built
for the War Office.

Exterior and interior views of a 2-ton long-wheelbase Ambulance built to War Office requirements. Modifications include special wheels and tyres, increased ground clearance, two petrol tanks and additional engine ventilation.

Part of the British Navy's land manoeuvres' fleet. The vehicles are standard long wheelbase trucks.

"For Service Overseas"

Built for the British Royal Air Force: a detachable canvas tilt body on the Bedford 30-cwt chassis. Note the increased bonnet ventilation.

A Bedford armoured car operated by the Japanese army in Manchukuo: and (right) a dual-purpose vehicle with detachable seats and racks for troop-carrying and general transport work in Malacca.

A specially designed army wagon on the 2-ton chassis for War Department use in the Near East.

"In Public Service"

Specially designed as a night-soil bucket carrier, these Bedfords,
with all-enclosed body, are operated by the Sanitary Authorities in
Suva, Fiji.

Hundreds of municipalities all over Great Britain use standard
Bedford municipal vehicles. Here is a 2-ton long wheelbase refuse
wagon owned by a London Corporation.

Part of a fleet of 46 Bedfords owned by the Utrecht Municipality.
The vehicles illustrated are refuse wagons with side 'steering
wheels' to operate the tipping gear.

Mounted on the 3-ton long chassis, this refuse tipping body has a
capacity of 15 cubic yards, a roller-shutter rear door, and a roller
floor with a load-compressing device.

"For Every Duty
Bedford Has The Answer"

From the humble dust cart to the gleaming fire engine, the Bedford range can provide a competitively priced vehicle for any municipal service. This 2-ton chassis has been bodied for a local fire brigade.

19

Above we see a fire engine on the 2-ton chassis specially equipped with foam extinguishers and other apparatus to deal with municipal aerodrome fires.

To carry all the emergency equipment required by this fire and rescue tender, the City of Johannesburgh opted for the heavy duty Bedford 3-ton chassis seen left.

A fire tender combining economy and practical utility. It is based on the standard 30-cwt truck, with lockers built into the body.

Smart and efficient-looking, this 2-ton fire engine carries a 350/400 gallon per minute pump, a 50ft wheeled escape and full first aid apparatus.

The modern 'limousine-type' fire tender. The example illustrated is on the 2-ton chassis. The crew and most of the equipment are carried inside.

"For Motoring Emergencies"

Sadly, not every vehicle is as reliable as a Bedford truck or a Vauxhall car, but when trouble strikes the reputable motor dealer knows that Bedford can lend a hand.

Here we have an example of a modern wrecking truck, or breakdown wagon, on the Bedford 3-ton chassis.

"Whatever The Job"

Special 'economy' ambulance, based on van body lines, and designed for public works departments, collieries and native hospital removals.

Keeping the country safe, and yet providing luxury for felons. A 30-seater prison van (Bedford bus chassis) built for service in Uganda. The interior comprises three separate compartments with sliding doors.

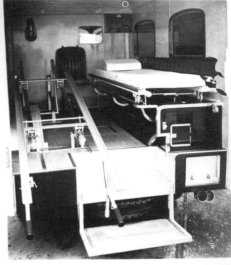

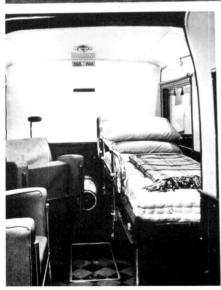

"Help Is At Hand"

Shown on the top left. the de-Luxe 30-cwt Ambulance, an extremely popular vehicle in the home market, and on the right, we have an interior view showing the easy loading device and the two-stretcher accommodation.

Interior of a special luxury ambulance for nursing home removals; and (right) a mines rescue van specially fitted for pit rescue work. Equipment includes fire-fighting apparatus, respirators, pumps, resuscitating outfit and life-lines.

"Moving Millions"

Part of a big fleet of Bedford buses and coaches operated by the Western Welsh Omnibus Co., Ltd.

Four 'native' buses with specially designed bodies and ventilation. They are used for a 25 mile service between Helouan and El Saff, in Upper Egypt.

"Station Wagons & Shooting Brakes"

A typical example of the estate-bus-cum-shooting-brake (top) in use on many big English country estates.

An extremely smart station coach supplied to hotels, to carry passengers and luggage to and from the railway station.

"Transport For Home
And Overseas"

This 20-seater "publicity" bus (top) carries a Swimming Cabaret all over England. This is a touring show sponsored by Eugene, of permanent wave fame.

A six-wheeler conversion with a special saloon coach body operated by the Danish State Railways.

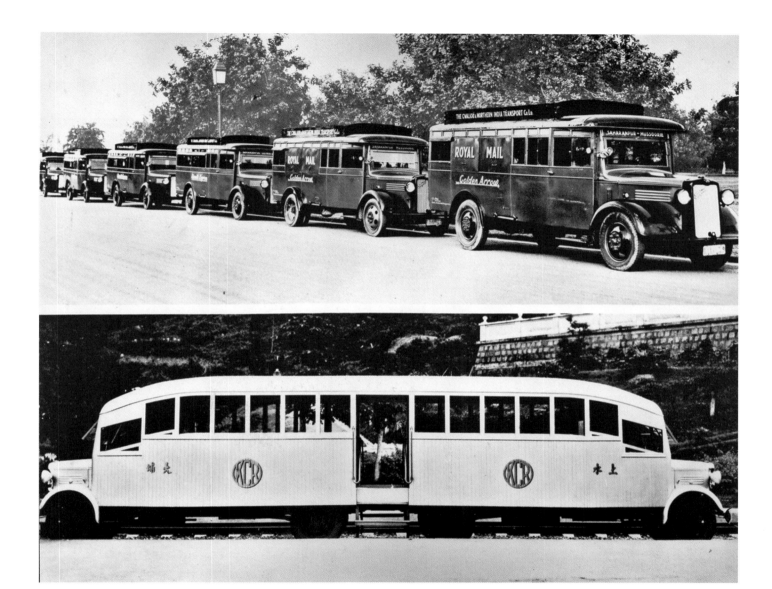

Operated by the Gwalior and Northern India Transport Co Ltd., these special buses are designed for part-passenger, part-Royal Mail loads.

Probably the most unusual Bedford in the world – a Chinese rail-car consisting of two 3-ton chassis mounted back to back with engine and controls at each end. Accommodation is for 34 passengers and luggage, and the 'vehicle' is in regular service as a train on the Kowloon-Canton Railway.

"Long Loads Over Great Distances"

The new Bedford-Scammell tractor and trailer unit. The platform body illustrated has a payload of 8-tons and is designed for a gross laden weight of 12-tons.

Hauling timber in New Zealand – a long wheelbase Bedford with a special trailer-bogy attachment in use in Otago.

30

Bagai Motor Service operate some 200 Bedfords on the North-West Frontier of India. The vehicle illustrated is a complete mobile service station fitted with compressor, spraying apparatus and so on. The interior view is of another Bagai service unit – a running repairs outfit with benches and comprehensive tool equipment.

An articulated Bedford with an aluminium bodied trailer extension used on long trunk-road service runs.

"Catering For All Tastes"

Hot and cold meals, drinks and snacks are supplied at race-meetings and other gatherings by the owner of this Bedford travelling restaurant.

A travelling 'fish and chips saloon' on the 30-cwt chassis (for country district trade) is seen top left and, top right, a complete travelling theatre which carries artistes in a saloon compartment at the front and 'props. in the back.

Bottom left: Built by a coach proprietor, this mobile hotel has accommodation for six people, kitchen, bath, bedrooms, lounge, electric light, hot and cold water, wireless set and cocktail bar! Bottom right: One of many Bedford travelling libraries put into service to cater for remote country districts.

"Specially Designed Body Work"

Travelling shop and cinema combined, this Church Army vehicle is used to display the work of disabled ex-Service men.

A de-luxe caravan, on an extended 30-cwt chassis, with an overall length of 23ft 6in. and a sun verandah built on to the tailboard.

Top left, a 5/6cwt show-van with window sides and announcement loudspeaker used for gift-coupon publicity: and (top right)A 30cwt van, one of a fleet operated by Harper's Automatics to carry slot-vending machines.

No need to enquire the owner's business in this case seen bottom left. The special body is on a Bedford 2-ton long chassis.

Bottom right: A living-van with bunk, desk, bookcase and etceteras, designed as a mobile advertising unit for a Scottish coach proprietor.

Top left: Deep side boards and extra loading height render this 3-tonner most suitable for the shop-fitting trade.

Top right: An example of modern streamlining – a Bedford laundry van (one of a fleet) operated by Collars Ltd.

Bottom left; E.R.A. (English Racing Automobiles) use several of these Bedford vans to convey cars and mechanics to English and Continental race-tracks.

Bottom right: A 6-door 8-seater Bedford which carries passengers and newspapers between Palmerston North and Wellington, New Zealand, 206 miles a day and always on time with the news.

Top left; A special display van used to demonstrate electrical motors to power companies and municipal undertakings.

Top right: A similar vehicle designed for demonstrations of paraffin cookers and heaters.

Bottom left: This articulated Bedford carries a demonstration air raid shelter round the country for a firm of builders and contractors.

Bottom right: An outsize pantechnicon used to carry complete sets of milking machinery to agricultural shows.

"The Sport Of Kings"

Built to carry three horses, this streamlined horse box has a
loading line only 21 inches above ground level.

For four horses, the "Horse-Coach", as this articulated vehicle
(shown below) is known, provides more than ample
accommodation.

"Sporting Achievements"

A 'hound and flesh cart' supplied to the Portman Hunt. The equipment includes a portable ramp for loading and unloading hounds.

A racing eight is over 60 feet long. This photograph shows how Tims of Oxford, famous Varsity boat-builders, solve the problem of road transport.

"From Tankers to Telegraph and from Churns to Bottles"

A special oil-tanker on the Bedford 3-ton long chassis, one of many operated by the manufacturers of Castrol.

Built for bulk haulage of liquids, this Towers Creameries tanker is mounted on the new articulated Bedford-Scammell.

Top: Exterior and interior views of a mobile post office used by the Danish postal authorities at race-meetings and public gatherings. A portable aerial is carried for morse telegraphy.

Bottom: One man's meat is another man's poison. The photographs show how beverages of different kinds are handled by two internationally known concerns.

"Special Applications"

This Bedford mobile crane is in use in a New South Wales steel works. The crane is removable. It is controlled by one man, and it handles loads from 2-cwt to 15-cwts.

A Bedford 3-tonner adapted for driving tuition for the British School of Motoring, and right a 30-cwt insulated bread van specially built for use in the Iran oilfields settlements.

One of the 1,700 Bedfords purchased by Pickfords, the famous carriers, in the last few years, and (right) a 2-tonner fitted up as a safari car for use in Kenya.

A powerfully-braced steel tipping body supplied for work in the Iran oilfields, with a cross-braced front gantry for pipe-carrying. Right: A 2-ton van with side roller shutter opening and side "tailboard".

"The Long And Short Of It"

The Bedford 5/6-cwt "Utilecon", a van-cum-passenger body for estate and general work. The interior view shows the disposition of the collapsible passenger accommodation.

Below: This 3-ton van body, with a 45" chassis extension, measures 20ft 6in inside. It is used to carry aircraft sections and tail-planes.

A laundry van body with down-swept rear panel and roller shutter door, typical of many in use in England: and (right) a specially ventilated and insulated van for carrying perishable foodstuffs

Two examples of unusual high head-room bodies built for special requirements. The 5/6-cwt ice-cream vehicle operates as a travelling stall. The Express van is designed to carry domestic and shop refrigerators.

"Famous Fleets"

There are big Bedford fleets in service all over the world. This picture shows a few of the 30-cwt vans owned by The Wonder Bakery.

In Afghanistan, nearly 500 Bedfords are at work carrying raw cotton from Mazara-Shariff to the nearest rail-head, seven days' journey away, over rugged country and primitive roads. The photograph is of some of the first 3-tonners to leave England for this arduous work.

*Typical examples of some of the big Bedford fleets in use in the
United Kingdom. The R. White mineral waters fleet totals nearly
200 vehicles. The sand and ballast lorries feed building estates
and factory sites over the whole of the Greater London area.*

Large fleets of road vehicles are run by the main British railway companies. Typical are these pictures of cattle wagons operated by the London and North Eastern Railway, and delivery vans and trucks in the service of the Southern Railway. Both organisations run several hundred Bedfords.

"Down On The Farm"

A side-loading egg-transporter on the 3-ton chassis, with tarpaulin weather sheets: and the Bedford 6-cwt Utility Wagon. The owner has rigged up a temporary "cage" for poultry.

Two vehicles designed for the agricultural industry – a cattle wagon with removable deck for pigs and sheep, and a market gardener's lorry with rack sides for high loading.

"Back To School"

Designed to carry 40 children, this Bedford school bus is mounted on the passenger chassis.

The interior of the school bus illustrated above. Various safety devices are fitted to doors and windows.

We finish as we began. Wherever there is a transport job to be done a Bedford can be sold to do it. In this picture, crated vehicles are being disembarked on to surf-boats to be paddled and manhandled to the Gold Coast beach at Accra. Truly, 'you see them everywhere'.

Author's Note: This remarkable collection of photographs, which has been miraculously saved for 65 years is, in all respect, a truly representative image of the Bedford range of vehicles in the late-1930s. However, both the photographs showing goods being landed by native boats are in fact photographic fakes, made up from several different images.

"You see them everywhere"

SOME WELL KNOWN USERS OF BEDFORDS

In the following list are the names of some of the internationally-known firms and organisations who rely on Bedfords. Most of them are extensive users of commercial vehicles, and several are operating Bedford fleets running into three and four figures.

War Office
Royal Air Force
Royal Navy

Afghanistan Government
Anglo American Oil Co.
Anglo Iranian Oil Co.
Anglo Dutch Petroleum Co.
Bagai Motor Service
Baird Television
Barclays Bank
Bovril
British Drug Houses
British Marine Aircraft
Cadbury's
Carreras
Castrol
Celanese
Cossor Radio
Daily Dispatch
Daily Express (London)
Daily Herald (London)
Daily Sketch (London)
Daimler Hire
Danish Bacon Co.
De Havilland Aircraft

Dewars Whisky
Elders & Fyffes
Evening News (London)
Evening Standard (London)
Express Dairy
Fifty Shilling Tailors
Firestone Tyres
Frigidaire
Fry's
Gaumont-British
General Electric Co.
General Steam Navigation Co.
Gillette
Golden Shred
Goodyear Tyres
Haig Whisky
Handley Page
Hartley's
His Masters Voice
Imperial Chemical Industries
International Broadcasting Co.
Jockey Club, Newmarket
Kodak
Lever Bros.
Liptons
London & North Eastern Railway
London County Council
Manchester Guardian
Marks & Spencer
Maple's
Metro-Goldwyn-Mayer
Metropolitan Water Board
Michelin Tyres
Milk Marketing Board
National Benzole Co.
National Cash Registers

News Chronicle (London)
Oxo
Pickfords
Ponds Extract
Racecourse Betting Control Board
Radio Times
Rangoon Tramways
Redline-Gilco
Regent Petrol
Remington
Rolls Royce
Schweppes
Shell Oil
W.H. Smith & Son
Southern Railway
The Star
St. John Ambulance Brigade
Stephens Ink
Tate & Lyle
Triplex Safety Glass
Vacuum Oil Co.
Vickers Armstrong Ltd.
Vickers Aviation
Virol
Waring & Gillow
White Label Whisky
R. White & Sons
Wolsey Underwear

(This list is not by any means a comprehensive one. In addition to many more "household names", hundreds of Government departments, municipalities, co-operative societies and public works authorities all over the world have been omitted.)